MADDENING MAST CELL MATHEMATICS:
A CHRONIC ILLNESS CALCULUS

MADDENING MAST CELL MATHEMATICS:

A CHRONIC ILLNESS CALCULUS

poems about life with ehlers-danlos and mast cell activation syndrome

Sarah Klein

QUERENCIA

Querencia Press - Chicago Illinois

QUERENCIA PRESS

© Copyright 2025
Sarah Klein
Cover Art: Mandy Lafond
All Rights Reserved

ISBN 978 1 959118 94 7

Cover Art: Mandy Lafond

www.querenciapress.com

First Published in 2025

Querencia Press, LLC
Chicago IL

Printed & Bound in the United States of America

CONTENTS

Preface

This is a book about my lifelong experience with hypermobile Ehlers-Danlos syndrome (EDS), a genetic disorder that impacts the production of collagen and mast cell activation syndrome (MCAS), a condition where the body's mast cells involved in immune and allergy response are hyperreactive. The two disorders are both massively underdiagnosed and underestimated in their capability to cause intense pain and fatigue along with other impairments. Disorders such as dysautonomia, Myalgic Encephalitis (ME/CFS), and small fiber neuropathy, among many others, are also often present and also woefully unaddressed in any medical system. Under global capitalism, this prejudice can stack with other factors of race, gender, sexuality, neurodiversity, and so on. Many people are misdiagnosed with "fibromyalgia" or written off entirely as hypochondriacs or as having a psychosomatic disorder. Needless to say, this exacerbates the stress of life with these conditions and causes its own trauma. My hope in sharing this book is that I will reach others who have experienced chronic illness so they know they are not alone. For those still waiting to be heard, I offer you my solidarity in suffering.

Neurologically adrift

My body buoyed up by quotidian needs
I rise, an overstuffed conduit,
A haywire conclave of desires
Under the aegis of a biomass
Too clumsy to concentrate,
Approximating its behavior
As a poor translation from
A much richer language:
Murdering metaphor and
Sequestering all into a
Misapplied vector—
I cajole the simulacrum
Through the hours
To signify me,
To transmit something
Like myself, among
Hampered and defunct
Connections, to speak
A language dribbled through
A flawed matrix—
It will do, Gödelian loop,
It will have to do

I did not survive

my very existence
is
maligned
denied
gaslit
a walking rind of
trauma
peeled away from a human being
my body a house on fire
and yet no one will spare a drop

I have to paint the hell
in words
to make you understand
because you cannot see me
you will not see me
in my agony,
clutched to my chest for years
but even when I brandished it
the battle left wounds in me
that seep into my nervous system
shorts in the circuit
and the dulled anger
comes back and roars
and roars and roars

I did not survive to be
ignored,
trampled,
forgotten

when it rains

when it rains my body gathers up all its trauma to twist it into a new shape spiky and silver. I want to look away but it shines like a beacon until my eyes are raw the rivers within me running red pumping madly to keep up and I am captive in its crumbling castle. dinner reeks of dread in tarnished teacups i swallow and swallow until I choke. agony arcs through me sudden and sharp I feel compressed into a cube of cascading candles burning my brain as I stomp them silent. to feed the flowers I throb and thrash my body rent into a rictus when it rains

inspiring!

inspiring! this young woman, (who is maybe not a woman but was squeezed too tight into the sleeve of femininity) who has felt the leaden weight of fatigue every day, whose nerves crackle and throb, whose muscles ache and scream, who was gaslit so many times it was an environmental crime, who cried alone from grief and then from pain and then from grief borne of pain, whose humanity was reduced to a number again and again, who was brushed aside like a buzzing fly, who stood up and pushed back because otherwise she could not face another day, who was lucky enough in some ways and neglected in others, whose life was a struggle that no one would acknowledge, who carved out the tiniest niche to have some peace and solace, who awakens in a world bent on killing her and crushing her and oppressing her and using her further—

she can write in a way (you can't even see her) crouched behind the screen with joints that slip and slide and stab and a spine that screams; she can write so beautifully that you will be surprised when you call her *inspiring* and she spits in your face

Post-Traumatic Mathematics

The matrix that is my mind
suspended as a program
I plait my diseased thoughts
into metallic braids, pulling
them close, a strand for
each acronym I am taxonomized
into, classifications of disorders,
names to explain myself to myself
lay language from the computing
engine that I can only change by
trial and error, partially deciphered
rosetta stone, the strands bound
up into helices, coding exons clacking,
all we have endeavored to find
still not sufficient to understand
under the knife the Gordian knot
simply sliced and studied but
the tangling perseveres, multiplies,
races ahead of my hurried notes,
swallows me whole from inside
magnificent and yet when you
tell me to trust it you are not aware
of just how quickly I am ensnared

Diagnosis

look at me,
I said, my chest open
to my tattered heart on
display, choking on my
lungs as if they had rolled
back in time into asthmatic
paroxysms, my hands shake
and my voice fractures, look
at me, please, I beg, and I break
and break and break, a china cup
thrown to the ground and glued back
together weaker every time, through tears
and white lies, through dismissals and refusals,
look at me, I pleaded, withering away from the
desire to persist at all, and I am lucky because one
day one of them looked at me sobbing and said,
I see you.

Look, Mom, I'm Chronically Ill

you who felt the vise so soon, the cold hand of death piercing
you with his bony finger, placing the blossom of fatality in your
breast, you who mourned your hair while your spirit broke
when it was the nanny teaching us to ride bikes, you who sat
up with me while the albuterol wound its way through my
airways, you who told me "try just a little bit longer" to go to
sleep, you who I feel through my bones because I remember
your anger, your fear that we were afraid of you bald, when it
was really that we could see the pain inside you when you
yelled, that life was pounding us to pieces and to disappoint
you was in itself a terror, you who fought and fought and
fought, you who died at eight years older than I am now, you
who gave me a plush dog for braving the orthodontist, please
do not be sad to know the shape I live in now, the experiences
of yours I shared, please know it is enough that you showed
yourself as a human being to us, in all your fear and anger and
sadness, there was so much loving, there was so much loving,
enough that it burst up through me to scream and thrash in
fury, enough so that I could keep on living, so that I could keep
on living for you

Your prior authorization has been denied

Say what you will
About man, about machine
I cannot live in automated distress.

A handshake in the cold
Is an algorithm waiting to unfold
The misery we see
Amplified and then distorted

A billion pairs of eyes
And a flick of a wrist

I cannot live in automated distress.

That we infuse
All that we use
With the original sin of our making:
The ex post facto,
The judicial argument,
The numbers counting up

That to be seen
Is not to be heard

I cannot live in automated distress.

There is no one
To wrench the tools from
That is not ourselves.

The faith that we will make
A better way

I can no longer
Distinguish from religion.

Something That Will Still Be Seen

Loss is the cording
That composes my bones
My skin stretched from birth
Around the genetic mutation
That makes me fold too far

By hyperextension
I twisted my inner world
To avoid, accommodate, acclimate
Being flexible came
So naturally and it was a talent
To treasure in the gaping absence
Of relating to any other child
I could be praised for it and
For the way I hid in books and facts
And functions of my brain
So much more brilliant than
Aching limbs and wheezing lungs and
Nervous tics

To stand firm, to survive
Was a foreign language learned on the fly
And I was forced to flex into it
And stay and it unraveled
All the years behind me so tightly bound
In loops and knots

In cords that connected me
Where ligaments failed

And every morning I wrap myself
In myself even as I fall apart, because
After all this time it is still easiest
To flex and flow and fit in the corners
To wind my way under the wallpaper to be
Something that will still be seen

Stain for CD117

it's my mast cells,
I will say, as underneath
the flushed skin my blood
bubbles & boils & churns,
the acid eroding my stomach
lining rises and chokes me
as my anger flares: my body
firing on all cylinders in distress—

the messily stitched-together
interweaving of a lived
experience with cells gone awry:
I want an autonomy I cannot
claim—and I channel it toward
my knowledge of the chemical
reactions in the cells that they
saw under microscope as
abnormal, hidden until the dye
brought them into the harsh
light of the clinical gaze, finally—

this I can understand and explain,
I can educate the way the trigger
works because what I have to
avoid is the buried part of me
that I know is *angry with cause,*

23

that I rein in, tame, smooth out,
make palatable, relatable,
shape into something that
people will read, nodding to
themselves, a rational frustration—

to keep what I view as a monster
from consuming me, even
though the monstrosity is the horror
of so many hours I have seen,
swallowed, agonized, cried, I
restrain myself so they will not
restrain me, they will not hear me:
fuck you, you did not believe me,
you saw me suffer and you filed
me away in a drawer under *hysterical*;
fuck you, you harmed me, the snake
on the rod of Asclepius should strangle
you until you feel the panic rise
within and set your whole body alight—
and that's your mast cells.

What Cannot Be Quantified Will Be Ignored

0: limbo. null and void. a distant memory long since archived. one moment, a breath, glimpsed but never revealed.

1: me, myself. the locus. brain in a jar. the only bystander, the sole victim. closed off in my experience like a gated lot.

2 plus 3 plus 2: hours. interruptions in a night of sleep, a mind sticking up into cognizance, a lashed animal urged onward.

3: years of stomach symptoms this go-around, months notched into a bedpost, patience burnt and brittle.

4: for others, not me. my four held up like a mirror reflects infinite possibilities for infinite pains. as if our fours could connect and make sense and average out into a dose. as if a mathematical equation could spell out *ache*.

5: should it be half ten? half of agony, neatly parceled like a shared cookie? i think earthquake, richter, logarithmic is more precise. five minutes, five business days. business as usual.

6: the edges of my mind become fuzzy. insistent pressure tamping down clarity. the hammering on the door is louder. heaviness seeps through my fragile skin into my bones.

7: a chronic-pain cerebral calculus: what number do you want? what will you believe? is my body too large, too young, to ascend to its rightful throne as acknowledged in suffering?

8: the worst time was when someone snapped at me, "so you're in severe pain now?" when i hazarded a "5". the best time was the nurse who suggested we update the scale to "how many times have you cried today?"

9: remembering at least it is easier to let go of life in this much pain. if this becomes my new reality, i won't be as afraid. all the medications, double the doses, whatever it takes.

10: parched in the desert. i pray for the roof to fall in on me and crush me to death

Brain Fog

Fatigue like you're haunting yourself
A threadbare version that falls apart
In a gust of a breath too deep or a spasm too hard
Thoughts and words fall away through a sieve
Leaving a husk that labors in vain

A free trial of aphasia
Like a virus downloaded into my dendrites
Spam filter broken, chaos rules:
The marvels of the machine beyond my reach

Suspended in static, I wail and writhe
Fists beat uselessly the tide
Sedate, soothe, medicate
Never look into the abyss
Of possibility that this is eternal
Despite every cell screaming what if what if what if

Detective Work

I read my shit in the toilet like a haruspex:
squinting, committing to memory its
shapes and colors to accord them with
aches, pains, gas, all the assorted wails
that echo through my body as my guts
reclaim itself from itself, autoinflammatory
trigger flipped on and let to burn, scalding
the villi like crisping leaves, the peculiar
ash left behind a native plant grown fat
on waste and choking out everything else

a forest does not grow back in
a day, or even a year, and neither
does a microbiome, and in the same
way that we control the burn of forests
but have few other solutions, I must
let a ravaged body take its time to
fight back with only a few pruning
tools, and left to my own devices,
forgotten about by even those
who once acknowledged me, I am
the sole warden in this landscape
and you'd track animals by their
waste so don't wrinkle your nose
like that in disgust, I am simply
gathering data toward homeostasis

Acrostic Through the Body

Hormone and neurotransmitter, so
Incredibly influential on my
State of mind, or mood, so quickly
That too much of it rushes through me,
Ambushed by the very cells keeping me alive,
Multi-functional and we cannot do without,
Illness as overblown protection mechanism,
Not unique in this way, I simply wish it did not creep into
Everything

Meditation on Eugenics

do not go gently you whose bones shrivel and warp, you whose guts churn and perforate, you who are missing your flesh, your organs, your mind: you who know the shuffling away, the categorization, the minimization, the torture, you who have suffered under the clinical gaze, the familial gaze, the white gaze, the male gaze, you who have been ignored, you who have had everything taken away

rage, rage against the taking of your life

Lost Lullaby

Like being lost in a maze of clouds
Locked away from myself
As though neurons were snapped,
Parts of my mind amputated

Like a lower-resolution copy
Of myself and all the language
I have nurtured so lovingly
Is ripped away from me and buried

A battering ram against these walls—
But I am so tired, and I know
I will only sap my strength.
I lay suspended in my numbness,
Waiting to wake up whole again.

Well, That's American Healthcare

Apologist apotropaic rituals:
"Do not ask for efficacy,
You already asked for action."

Modern-age machines:
Easier to show horror,
Easier to just ignore.

The patterns of history
Remain inscrutable
With eyes closed—

Or they are heralded
As fixed, beyond intervention,
As if in god-paradox
We built a society
We couldn't fix.

You can hide from us
But you cannot deny
Your comfort is our deaths
Which is why you cannot stand
To hear us scream

My Body the Union

My body the union
Going on strike

Involuntary scab:
I have to exist

Space-time break
A prescription
Never in stock

My anger ricocheting
Between myself and the world

Oh do not mistake my fury
For lack of care.

Oh do not mistake
My lack of care
For lack of fury.

Autonomics Trumps Logic Equation

A Moravec's paradox of neurotransmission:
Drawing logic lines from chemistry
And lived experience points to my distress
Being heavily mediated by a reaction
Linked to my somatic condition—

But I cannot feel any different, cannot
Stop the mood laying its heavy blanket over me
Can hardly control the symptoms
Swelling up from within to swallow me.

Wear A Fucking Mask

Paper-thin I spread myself
Far enough to cover an axiomatic relevance
You have taken it all for granted, plundered
Your own vitality like it was an old-fashioned treasure chest,
hasp hanging, in ignorance of the curse that runs beneath the
sinew and skin, and when you are recalled to observe frailty
and fracture you scald your eyes on it, your steel stomach
turns, you brain curls up inside the comfort of cognitive
dissonance, and others would taunt you with your own decay,
hold a mirror to your face and draw the lines upon it, an appeal
to the hollow selfishness in which you have deigned to, brick
by brick, build your abode, I will simply grow into the space
you made for yourself, orbit you and at my perihelion shatter
myself, pieces wide and far, the misery written into me, and
make you look upon it, wedge myself in your soft eyeball, a
sledgehammer of a metaphor for you who will not open your
doors of perception to my agony—my art

I Have Not Yet Even Begun

Every day the demiurge
Coming clearer and clearer into view
Honing my teleology, holding in my guts,
Collecting the detritus of the fallen,
Plotting heaven and hell on the graph, asymptotes shifting,
opening up dimensions,
The picture slips, wrinkles, bleeds, the world
Tilts, shakes, seethes, patterned violence
Permeating so thoroughly I cannot
Acknowledge the ignorant without bubbling inside, occult
fractures like popcorn bursting through my bones, you thought
I was bellicose before and I have not even begun to fight

Proprioception: the sense of the body in space

impaired
I am adrift
a leaf in the wind

when your body
is against mine
I can feel you
and me through you

I am grounded
by your touch
physically and metaphysically

you give life to
my form
your presence
allows my mannequin-body
to move, lets me puppet
the clumsy cage my heart is locked inside

oh, to throw my doll-arms around you

Notes on Prior Publication

"Stain For CD117" was originally published in the August 2023 edition of Lammergeier.
https://www.lammergeier.org/post/two-poems-sarah-klein

"What Cannot be Quantified Will Be Ignored" was originally published in "Reformatting the Pain Scale" print anthology by Olney Magazine.

www.ingramcontent.com/pod-product-compliance
Lightning Source LLC
Chambersburg PA
CBHW071547120626
46550CB00006B/2607